JUPITER

Planet Guides

JUPITER

Duncan Brewer

MARSHALL CAVENDISH
NEW YORK · LONDON · TORONTO · SYDNEY

Library Edition Published 1992

Published by Marshall Cavendish Corporation
2415 Jerusalem Avenue
PO Box 587
North Bellmore
New York 11710

Series created by Graham Beehag Book Design

Library of Congress Cataloging-in-Publication Data

Brewer, Duncan, 1938-
   Jupiter/ Duncan Brewer,
     p. cm. - (Planet guides.)
   Includes index.
   Summary: Examines the physical characteristics and conditions of Jupiter, describing its position in relation to the Sun and other planets and surveying humanity's attempts to penetrate its mysteries.
   ISBN 1-85435-368-3 (set) ISBN 1-85435-373-X
   1. Jupiter (Planet) - Juvenile literature. [1. Jupiter (Planet)] I. Title.
   II. Series: Brewer, Duncan, 1938- Planet guides.
   QB661.B74 1990   90-40812
   523.4'5 – dc20   CIP
                             AC

Printed in Singapore by Times Offset Pte Ltd
Bound in the United States by Worzalla Publishing Co.

SAFETY NOTE

Never look directly at the Sun, either with the naked eye or with binoculars or a telescope. To do so can result in permanent blindness.

Acknowledgement

Most of the photographs, maps and diagrams in this book have been kindly supplied by NASA.

Title Page Picture:
The face of Jupiter, its moon Io is seen in transit in front of the planet in this Voyager picture.

Contents

Jupiter, the Gas Giant

Next to Jupiter, the other planets of the Solar System shrink into insignificance. It has more than twice the mass of all the other planets and their moons put together. Despite its great distance from the Earth – its average distance from the Sun is 483,600,000 miles (778,300,000 kilometers) compared to Earth's 93,000,000 miles (150,000,000 kilometers) – Jupiter outshines all the other planets in our night sky except for brilliant Venus – the morning and evening star. Venus may be brighter, but Jupiter is visible for far longer. It can hang high in the sky throughout the night and shines brightly for most of the year. Even the ancient astronomers recognized Jupiter as something special.

Senior planet of the Solar System, Jupiter's true face was unknown to early astronomers. Their instruments could not see the brilliant bands and spots shown by this Voyager image.

Jupiter or Jove, the supreme Roman god (Zeus to the Greeks), was the son of Saturn whom he is shown dethroning in this 18th century illustration. Jupiter was called Lord of Heaven and the bringer of light. He is holding lightning in his right hand.

They could not have known how enormous the planet is, but they still named it after the king of the gods. The ancient Hindus named the planet 'Dyaus Pitar,' or Father of Heaven, which became 'Jupiter' in Roman times.

New Moons

The Italian astronomer, Galileo Galilei, and a German astronomer, Simon Marius, both studied Jupiter through crude telescopes in the first decade of the seventeenth century. Galileo is credited with discovering the four major moons of the planet, though Marius probably found them at about the same time. Galileo wrote about this and other telescopic discoveries he had made in his book, *Sidereus Nuncius (The Sidereal Messenger)*, which was published in 1610. In the second week of January that year, Galileo had seen first three, then four, tiny, star-like points of light close to Jupiter. Watching their movements from one night to the next, Galileo came to the conclusion that they were small 'starry' bodies orbiting the planet. His telescope was not powerful enough to show the moons as little disks. He saw only points of light, similar to those which stars present to our most powerful present-day telescopes.

Church Resistance

Marius named the four satellites in order of increasing distance from Jupiter. Their names were Io, Europa, Ganymede and Callisto, four of the mythological characters associated with the king of the gods. Nowadays we refer to them as the Galilean moons or satellites, in honor of their discoverer. The Italian astronomer's great achievement was not just that he saw them through his primitive telescope, but that he realized how important they were in his arguments about the nature and form of the Solar System. The Catholic Church taught that the Earth was the center of all motion. Jupiter and its moons showed beyond a shadow of a doubt that there could be more than one center of rotation in the universe. Church members were stubborn in their beliefs. Some refused to believe Galileo. They preferred to deny, without any proof, what he knew to be scientifically true.

The discovery of the Galilean satellites also enabled a later astronomer, Ole Römer of Denmark, to make a remarkably accurate estimate of the speed of light. He compared satellite phenomena, such as eclipses, at various stages in Jupiter's orbit.

Short Days, Long Year

It takes Jupiter 11·86 Earth years to make one complete circuit of the Sun. The planet spins on its axis extremely fast for its size. It completes one rotation roughly every 9 hours 55 minutes, so that one of Jupiter's years covers about 10,500 of its days. Earth and Mars both have axes that tilt markedly from the

This image taken from above the level of Jupiter's North Pole illustrates the flattened shape of the planet, caused by its high speed of rotation.

plane of their orbits to cause the four seasons in each hemisphere, owing to the varying exposure of any one place to the Sun's rays. Jupiter's axis tilts only a little – about 3°– so that there are no seasons on the giant planet.

Large-Scale Worlds

Jupiter, the first of the four *gas giants*, or Jovian planets, marks the beginning of the outer Solar System. Its distance from the Sun varies considerably due to its elliptical orbit, from 460,000,000 miles (740,000,000 kilometers) at *perihelion*, to 507,000,000 miles (816,000,000 kilometers) at *aphelion*. In addition to Jupiter, the other three gas giants – Saturn, Uranus and Neptune – are all many times larger and more widely spaced than the terrestrial planets – Mercury, Venus, Earth and Mars – which are tiny and closely bunched by comparison.

The terrestrial planets are small, solid and rocky. They also have differentiated structures. *Differentiation* occurred after they had congealed from the dust and gases of space. The terrestrial planets grew hotter as a result of internal pressures, the impacts of meteorites and friction. In some cases the immense heat generated melted the solid materials. Heavy materials became concentrated in the cores of the planets, forming metallic centers. In Earth's case, the hot core material has remained molten, or partly liquid. Lighter materials floated toward the surfaces of the planets. They hardened there, as they cooled, to become crusts.

Primal Gases

The Jovian planets of the outer Solar System also have solid cores, but the bulk of their substance is gas, principally hydrogen in various forms. The intense heat of the Sun at the center of the evolving Solar System dispersed many of the gases and lighter elements from the region of the terrestrial planets toward the outer

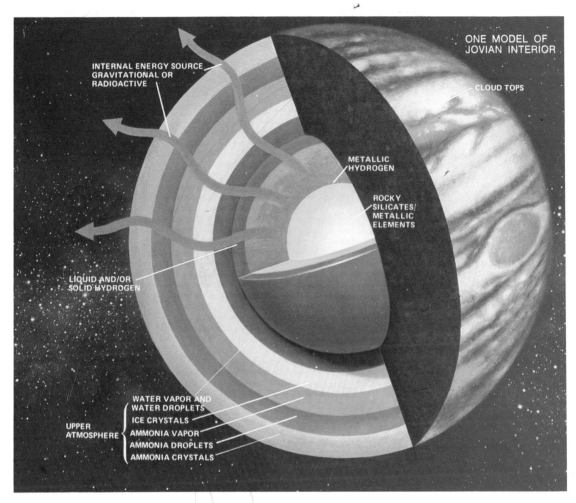

ONE MODEL OF
JOVIAN INTERIOR

INTERNAL ENERGY SOURCE
GRAVITATIONAL OR
RADIOACTIVE

CLOUD TOPS

METALLIC
HYDROGEN

ROCKY
SILICATES/
METALLIC
ELEMENTS

LIQUID AND/OR
SOLID HYDROGEN

WATER VAPOR AND
WATER DROPLETS
ICE CRYSTALS
AMMONIA VAPOR
AMMONIA DROPLETS
AMMONIA CRYSTALS

UPPER
ATMOSPHERE

The temperature at Jupiter's core may be as high as 54,000°F (30,000°C). It is surrounded by a deep layer of metallic hydrogen, created in conditions of enormous heat and pressure which are impossible to reproduce in Earth laboratories.

Solar System. The rocky lumps that became the primitive planets held on to some of the surrounding atmospheric gases. The tiny terrestrial planets, close to the Sun's heat, were not very successful at hanging on to gases. The outer planets, on the other hand, were very efficient. They grew much larger than the terrestrials, and they held on to the more widely available light gases in the outer regions of the Solar System.

Core Under Pressure

Jupiter itself was the most efficient of all the planets. It may have mopped up as much as 90 per cent of all the material that was available in the infant Solar System for planet formation. This material was compressed into Jupiter's present shape, a sphere with a diameter of 89,000 miles (143,000 kilometers). At its core, Jupiter has a densely compressed center of heavy elements, including metals and silicon. This core has 10 to 15 times the mass of Earth. The temperature of the core is in the region of 54,000°F (30,000°C). High though this is, it is nowhere near high enough to cause a nuclear reaction that could turn the planet into a star. The pressure at the center may be as high as 50,000,000 bars, or Earth atmospheres. Earth's core pressure is around 4,000,000 bars.

Liquid Metal Gas

Jupiter's core has a diameter of about 7,500 miles (12,000 kilometers). From the core outward, to a distance about 12,500 miles (20,000 kilometers) from the surface, there is a form of liquid hydrogen that has never been seen, even in a laboratory, on Earth. The

GALILEVS GALILEI FLORENTINVS
ANNVM AGENS LXXVIII

Galileo was the first truely modern scientist. He made important advances in both astronomy and mechanics. He observed that Jupiter had moons circling round it in much the same way that Copernicus had said that the Earth revolved round the Sun. Galileo's support of the Copernican theory made him enemies amongst those who still believed that the Earth was the center of the universe. In 1632 Galileo argued that the Copernican theory was correct. For this he was brought before the Court of the Holy Inquisition, and under the threat of torture, was forced to retract his opinions.

pressure and extremely high temperatures of the giant planet compress the hydrogen molecules. The compression is so great that the gas takes on a form known as *metallic hydrogen*. In this liquid state, the gas is electrically conductive.

Above the liquid metallic hydrogen is another layer. This is still hydrogen, and still liquid, but in a different form. In the region where the metallic hydrogen merges into the molecular hydrogen, the temperature may be about 20,000°F (11,000°C). Above the layer of liquid molecular hydrogen comes the planet's gaseous atmosphere, which is 625 miles (1,000 kilometers) deep. The temperature at the top of the visible atmosphere is about −240°F (−150°C).

The long, dark streak near the top of this image indicates a gap in the upper cloud layers. Pioneer 10, which flew past Jupiter in December 1973, took the first pictures showing that the planet's visible cloud layers are located at different altitudes.

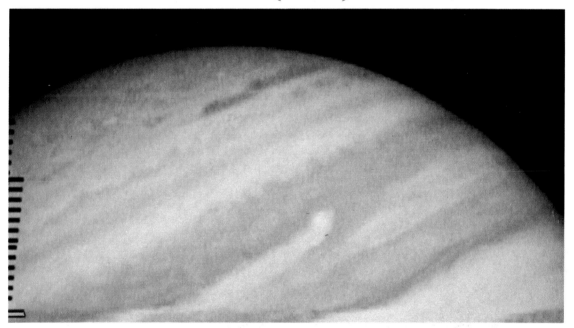

Low-density Giant

When we look at Jupiter through a telescope, we do not see a solid, rocky sphere like a terrestrial planet. We see the cloud tops in the planet's gaseous atmosphere. Except for its solid center, the sphere of Jupiter is made of liquid and gas. As a result, Jupiter's huge volume could hold more than 1,300 Earths, but the planet's average density is only 1·33 times that of water. Earth's density is 5·5 times that of water.

No Escape

Because of its great size and its distance from the warming rays of the Sun, almost all of Jupiter's substance stays with the planet instead of being lost out into space. Its huge size contributes to a surface gravity which is 2·64 times that of Earth. The planet's *escape velocity* – the minimum speed at which any matter must move in order to escape from Jupiter's atmosphere and gravity – is 128,700 mph (207,000 km/h) per second. Earth's escape velocity is only 24,840 mph (40,320 km/h). The extreme cold of the planet's upper atmosphere, at around −240°F (−150°C), lowers the speed of activity of atoms and molecules. The result is that Jupiter still has a hold on most of its original components. So one of Jupiter's fascinations for scientists is that it gives them the chance to study the materials from which the Solar System was formed 4·6 billion years ago.

Crystal Cloak

Jupiter, like the other gas giants, has a thick atmosphere. Most of it, about 86%, is hydrogen, while another 13·8% is helium. That leaves about 0·2% for all the other constituents. This matter includes 0·09% methane,

This artist's representation shows all four of Jupiter's Galilean moons: (left to right), Callisto, Europa, Io, and Ganymede. All were named by Simon Marius, a German astronomer who probably saw them at almost the same time as Galileo.

0·02% ammonia, and maybe 0·008% water vapor. These last three gases are what we see when we look at Jupiter through a telescope. They exist in ice-crystal or droplet form as dense clouds and give the planet its exterior appearance.

The atmosphere also includes a number of trace elements which exist in minute quantities. The main ones are ethane, acetylene, phosphine, carbon monoxide, hydrogen cyanide, germane, propane, and methyl acetylene.

Flat Spin

Galileo's first telescopes were good enough to see the four largest moons, but could not distinguish any surface markings on the planet itself. By the 1660s, many astronomers had seen the four Galilean satellites of Jupiter. With improved telescopes, the features of the planet became more distinct. By timing the movement of spots, scientists were able to establish the rotation period with reasonable accuracy at about ten hours. We now know that Jupiter rotates so fast that it flattens at the poles and swells outward around the equator. The equatorial rotation rate is faster than the rate at higher latitudes. Different rates of rotation occur at different points on the sphere. This is possible because Jupiter is a ball made largely of gases and liquids. The only solid part of the planet is its core.

At the equator, Jupiter makes a complete rotation approximately once every 9 hours and 50 minutes (Earth time). North or south at a latitude of about 10°, the rotation rate is about 9 hours and 56 minutes.

Striped Sphere

The improved telescopes of the late seventeenth century showed distinct bands running across the disk of Jupiter, parallel to the planet's equator. These bands of color alternated between light and dark. Astronomers now call the light-colored bands "zones," and the dark ones "belts." They are clouds of different gases which spread out around the planet as it spins. The bands also occur at differing altitudes. The bright zones are made of ammonia crystals massed in clouds at an altitude of between 50 and 60 miles (80 and 100 kilometers) where the atmospheric pressure is between 0·5 and 1 Earth atmosphere. About 20 miles (30 kilometers) closer to the planet are the belts of dark cloud, which consist of ammonium hydrosulfide crystals. Another 12 miles (20 kilometers) or so below the dark clouds are blue clouds of frozen water crystals.

Color Chemistry

Sulfur in the ammonium hydrosulfide causes the dark orange-brown shades of the belts. Red coloring is visible in some of the turbulence features, particularly in the southern hemisphere of the planet. It probably comes from phosphine brought up to the cloud surfaces by storm-like currents and turned into red phosphorus by the action of ultraviolet radiation from the Sun.

Convection currents in Jupiter's atmosphere are powered by heat from within the planet itself, not by the heat of the Sun. The bright zones mark the regions where heated gases rise up from below. As they cool down enough to form ammonia crystals, they sink. The dark belts mark the regions of cold, descending gas.

The Great Red Spot

In 1664, a British astronomer, Robert Hooke, reported seeing a great oval blemish in Jupiter's southern hemisphere. Other astronomers, such as Giovanni Cassini, the first observer to measure Jupiter's rotation period, also noticed what is now known as the Great Red Spot at about the same time as Hooke.

Since the two Voyager space probes flew close to Jupiter in 1979, we know that the Great Red Spot is the center of a huge storm. It is similar to a hurricane, but without an "eye." Like a great whirlwind, the Great Red Spot sucks up material from lower levels of the atmosphere, rotating counterclockwise about once every 6 Earth days. The Great Red Spot also protrudes about 5 miles (8 kilometers) above the top cloud level.

Jupiter's Great Red Spot is a huge storm system that has existed for centuries, rotating between counter-flowing bands of cloud, like an eddy in a giant river.

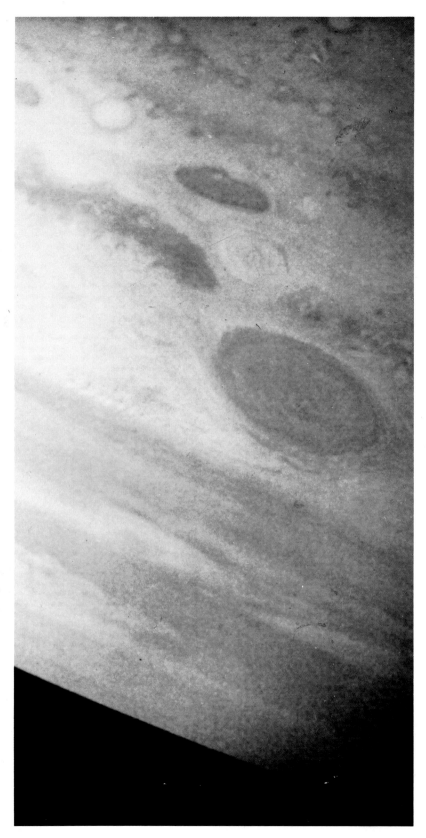

This view of Jupiter
taken from Pioneer 10 on
December 6, 1973,
shows the phase that is
never visible from Earth.
The Great Red Spot
appears as a regular
shape and is very
prominent.

This picture taken from
Voyager 1 in January,
1979 shows the planet as
being much more active.
The Great Red Spot
shows a much more
complicated structure.

The Great Red Spot is roughly oval, with its longest axis parallel to the planet's equator. The length of the Great Red Spot varies from 15,000 to 25,000 miles (24,000 to 40,000 kilometers), and its width stays constant at about 8,000 miles (13,000 kilometers). It varies in color between grayish-pink and bright red.

Great Red Puzzle

There have been many attempts to explain the Great Red Spot over the years. Some scientists thought it could be a solid "island" floating in Jupiter's upper atmosphere. Others thought it might be an area

This artist's impression shows how Jupiter's Great Red Spot may appear to an observer standing on Amalthea, Jupiter's most distant moon.

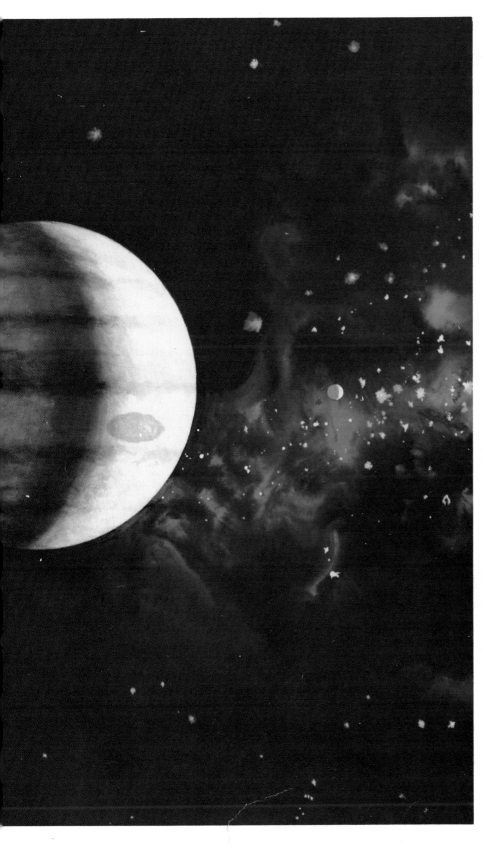

The Voyager probes brought new levels of technical sophistication to planetary exploration. Reaching Jupiter in March and July 1979, the two spacecraft produced the most brilliant and detailed images ever made of the giant planet.

After studying Jupiter and taking a close look at the Galilean moons, the two identical Voyager spacecraft used Jupiter's gravity to help them accelerate and change course for Saturn.

of turbulence and escaping gas hovering permanently above a volcanic feature or a mountain. We now know that Jupiter does not have any solid features. Also, the Great Red Spot does not stay in exactly the same position relative to the planet's "surface." It circles the planet slowly and erratically. It has made as many as three complete circuits of the planet over a period of thirty years. However, it has no recognizable

The moon Io, the major source of charged particles in the vicinity of Jupiter, is connected to Jupiter by the magnetic force-lines of its flux-tube (shown top right). The Voyagers were protected from the effects of radiation by special shields.

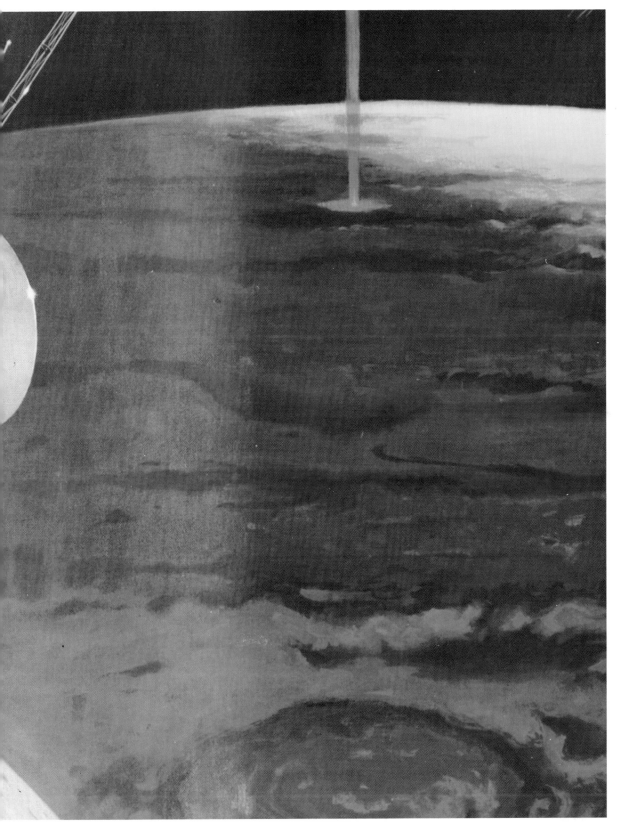

long-term cycle and has been known to stay in roughly the same position for thirty years at a time.

In the 1880s, the Great Red Spot was especially large. Astronomers described it as bright and brick-red. Over the next decade, it seemed to fade. It became almost invisible and then returned in the 1890s. The Great Red Spot is now only about half as long as it was in the 1880s. But it is still large enough to contain two Earths, side by side. Infrared measurements have revealed that the temperature at the top of the Great Red Spot is

Voyager revealed a world of constant motion in Jupiter's atmosphere. Spots rotate, bands of cloud circle the planet, and, in between, a maze of currents, spirals and vortices seethes.

−231°F (−146°C), which is 4°F (2°C) lower than the clouds around it.

Atmospheric Close-up

In March 1979, pictures of the Great Red Spot were relayed back to Earth from the Voyager 1 spacecraft. They showed that the rotating spot was pulling in material from the regions surrounding it at a rate of about 300 feet (100 meters) per second. This material circulated within the Great Red Spot for days. Then it was ejected violently, eastward and westward, into the counter-flowing currents that are responsible for the Great Red Spot and other, smaller, spots which are features of Jupiter's turbulent visible "surface." Voyager was able to identify gases, such as ethane and hydrogen cyanide, in the Great Red Spot, as well as the phosphine which wells up in the vortex from the lower atmosphere. As it becomes exposed to the powerful ultraviolet radiation bathing the planet above the cloud cover, the phosphine turns into red phosphorus.

Shrinking Spots

There are other, smaller spots rotating between the fast-moving currents of Jupiter's atmosphere. Three large, white ovals, each the size of Mars, have been observed south of the Great Red Spot for at least fifty years. These white ovals appeared in 1939, when each was almost 65,000 miles (100,000 kilometers) long. Since then, they have shrunk to around a tenth of that size.

Radio Jupiter

In the 1950s, American astronomers, working on a *radio frequency map* of the sky, by chance detected radio waves emanating from Jupiter. Further investigations with radio telescopes established that the planet was the source of varying types of radio waves. This was the first time that any planet other than Earth had been found to produce such radiation at radio wavelengths.

They were not radio messages, transmitted by intelligent beings, but emissions that occur naturally. The first radio radiation detected from Jupiter came in short, powerful, but irregular bursts. It is called *decametric radiation* and has wavelengths varying from 25 to 2,200 feet (7·5 to 670 meters). At much shorter wavelengths, between 2 inches and 10 feet (5 centimeters and 3 meters)', is a much more even, continuous emission of radio waves, known as *decimetric radiation*. At the

lowest end of this shortwave radiation is *thermal radiation,* with a wavelength generally shorter than 2¾ inches (7 centimeters).

As its name suggests, thermal radiation is caused by energy emissions related to the heat of an object or source. Jupiter's thermal radiation comes from the body of the planet, and measuring it has helped scientists to build up a picture of the structure of Jupiter's deeper layers of atmosphere, where telescopes and space probes cannot see. However, astronomers found that much of the decimetric radio noise came from a huge region around the planet. These emissions had nothing to do with Jupiter's temperature. They were too

Our own planet shrinks into insignificance compared to Jupiter. The Great Red Spot could hold three Earths. A century ago, the spot was twice as large as it is now.

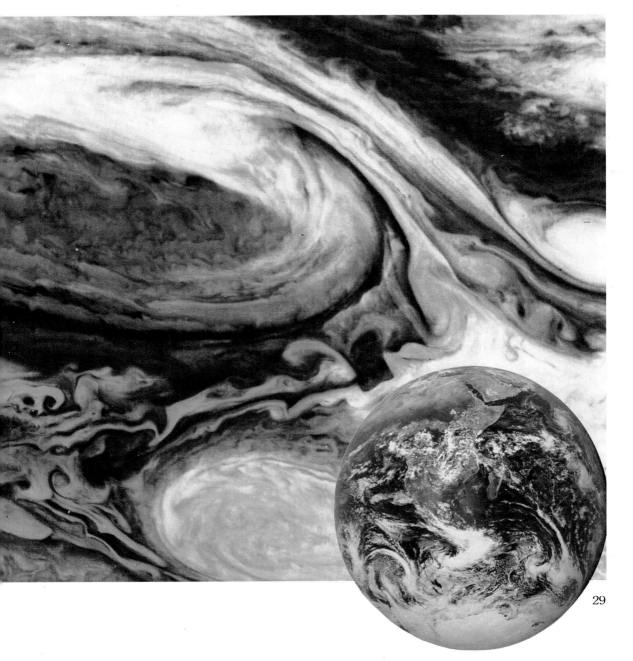

far from the center of the planet. The scientists concluded that they must be caused by the action of fast-moving charged particles on the force lines of a huge magnetic field.

Io on the Air

The powerful bursts of the longer-wave decametric radio emissions from Jupiter can last for a few minutes or a few hours. There are usually long inactive periods in between. Some of these radiation bursts may be due

Voyager took this image of the moon Io on March 2 1979. Later sequences of images proved that Io is volcanically active, with great plume eruptions jetting hundreds of miles into space.

to intense electromagnetic activity, such as lightning flashes in Jupiter's cloudy atmosphere. However, observers have also established that the intensity of the decametric radiation is closely related to the position in its orbit of Io, the closest of the four Galilean satellites.

The *magnetosphere* is the region around a planet in which its magnetic field has a significant effect on any particles it encounters. Jupiter's magnetosphere has a long, trailing teardrop shape. Its extended, tapering *magnetotail* streams away behind the planet, on the opposite side from the Sun. It reaches beyond the orbit of Saturn, the next of the Gas Giant planets.

Solar Windpower

The Earth's magnetosphere is similar in shape to that of Jupiter, but it is relatively smaller, taking into account the difference in size between the two planets. Also, the size of Earth's magnetosphere is stable. Jupiter's magnetosphere varies enormously in size, specifically in the direction of the Sun. Sometimes, Jupiter's magnetosphere streams toward the Sun to measure about 50 times its own radius. At its most extended, it reaches 100 Jupiter-radii toward the Sun. These variations are governed by the prevailing strength of the "solar wind." This constant stream of particles, mainly electrons and protons, emanates from the Sun. Its intensity varies according to the level of magnetic storm activity on the Sun, which follows an eleven-year cycle.

The magnetosphere is invisible to our eyes. If we could see it, it would appear as a huge envelope completely dwarfing Jupiter. From Earth, Jupiter's magnetosphere would look as large as the Sun.

Opposite: The Pioneer space probes, one of which is shown leaving the Earth-Moon system in this composite picture, acted as scouts for the later *Voyager* missions.

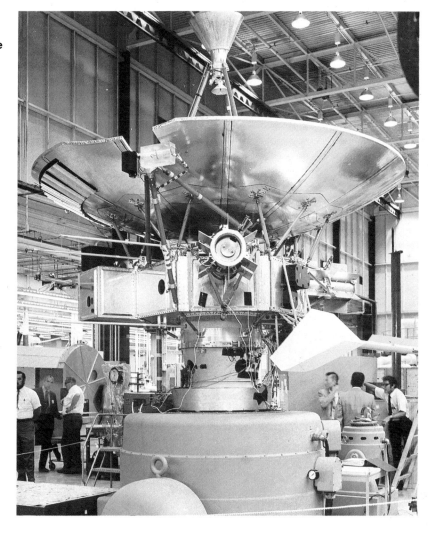

Right: Pioneer, seen here during testing, was not equipped with heavy-duty radiation shields. It suffered some instrument damage when it passed through the region of Jupiter's charged-particle torus, or ring.

Active Satellite

Charged particles interact with Jupiter's magnetic field to cause radio emissions. They come from three main sources. The solar wind itself is one, and the planet's ionosphere, a region of its atmosphere where the Sun's radiation creates free electrons and ions, is another. However, the main source of charged particles is the satellite, Io. Its volcanoes pour out almost a ton of heavy particles, including sulfur and oxygen, every second. These particles are ions, atoms which have been stripped of one or more of their electrons. This material from Io, escaping from its volcanoes as great jets of dust and sulfur dioxide, combines into a huge ring, or *torus,* around Jupiter, following Io's orbit. The radiation of the heavy ions in the torus would be fatal to any astronaut exposed to it. The first space probe to pass close to Jupiter, Pioneer 10, received a radiation dose of 200,000 *rads* from electrons, and 56,000 rads from protons. A 500-rad whole-body dose would kill a person.

Spacecraft and their delicate instruments are also very vulnerable to such intense bombardment, and the later Voyager probes were equipped with special radiation shields.

High-Voltage Surface

In addition to orbiting its parent planet within the doughnut-shaped torus, the satellite Io is constantly connected to Jupiter by a loop of magnetic field force lines known as a *magnetic flux tube*. This cluster of

The Pioneer spacecraft rotated five times a minute to keep it stable. This movement meant the images it produced were not as precise as those from the later Voyager probes. Pioneer's radio signal had a power of only 8 watts, and transmissions took 45 minutes to reach Earth.

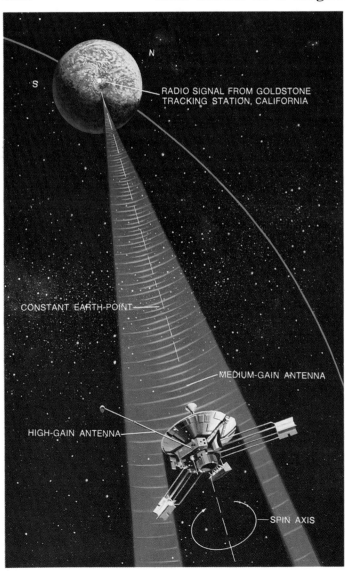

N

S

RADIO SIGNAL FROM GOLDSTONE TRACKING STATION, CALIFORNIA

CONSTANT EARTH-POINT

MEDIUM-GAIN ANTENNA

HIGH-GAIN ANTENNA

SPIN AXIS

field lines carries a massive electric current — up to 5,000,000 amps — and can discharge a potential 400,000 volts. This charge builds up on Io's surface as it orbits through the planet's magnetosphere. Its intense electromagnetic activity causes the sudden bursts of radio waves in the decametric range.

Magnetic Shockwave

The solar wind strikes the sun-side boundary of Jupiter's magnetosphere at a particle speed of some 930,000 miles (1,500,000 kilometers) an hour. At the boundary between the incoming pressure of the solar wind and the outward pressure of the magnetosphere, there is a

Pictured here above the Great Red Spot, Pioneer 11 safely crossed the asteroid belt between Mars and Jupiter. Eventually, it came close enough to Jupiter to be pushed by gravity toward Saturn.

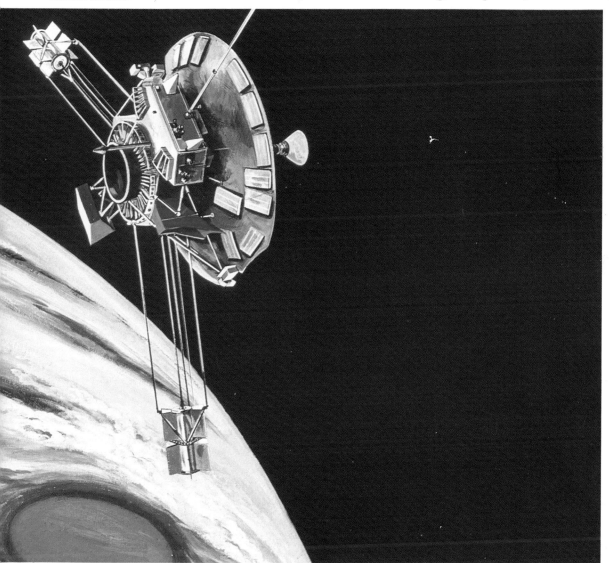

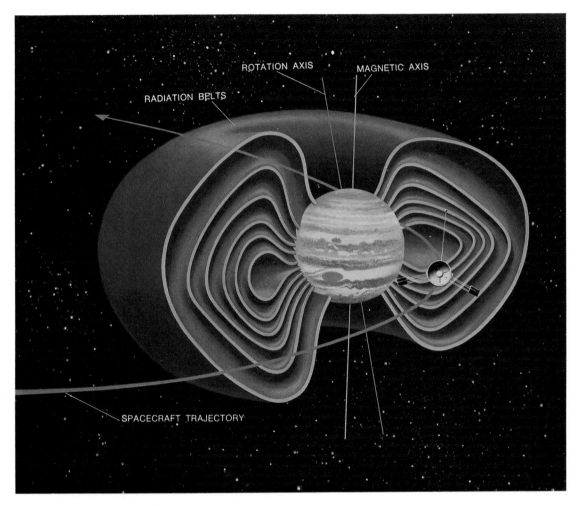

Within the image:
RADIATION BELTS
ROTATION AXIS
MAGNETIC AXIS
SPACECRAFT TRAJECTORY

shockwave known as the *bow-shock*. Inside is a region of great turbulence known as the *magnetosheath*. As the incoming particles of the solar wind strike the resistance of the bow-shock, they are slowed down dramatically, from 930,000 mph (1,500,000 km/h) to 250,000 mph (400,000 km/h).

Jupiter's magnetosphere is the region of space occupied by the planet's magnetic field. The outer magnetosphere varies in diameter from 4,400,000 to 13,200,000 miles (7,100,000 to 21,250,000 kilometers).

Hot Particles

This sudden slowing down has a remarkable effect on the electrons and protons of the solar wind. It increases their "effective temperature" by as much as 1,000 per cent making them hotter than the hottest regions of the Sun.

However, despite the enormous effective temperature of the individual particles, they are widely spaced in the massive reaches of the magnetosphere. So, the heat energy in any particular area of the magnetosheath as a whole is not remarkable. Thus, despite encountering the highest temperatures in the Solar System,

Pictures of Jupiter that were sent back to Earth by Pioneers 10 and 11 were made up of a limited series of overlapping images. The picture information was transmitted in digital form and computers on Earth translated the information into pictures.

space probes can pass unharmed through Jupiter's magnetosheath, to enter the magnetosphere through its outer limit, or *magnetopause*.

Jupiter's magnetosphere rotates with the planet, completing one rotation every 9 hours, 55 minutes, and 30 seconds. Scientists regard this time as the standard rotation period for the whole planet, though the visible planet shows a differential rotation, with different rotation periods at different latitudes.

Danger Zones

With Jupiter's huge magnetosphere rotating at such a high speed, enormous *centrifugal forces* compress the charged particles. They form a flattened sheet, called the *current sheet*, which extends away from the planet close to the plane of its magnetic equator. Jupiter's *magnetic axis* is tilted by 11° from the planet's axis of rotation, so its magnetic equator is tilted by 11° from its actual equator. The current sheet adds to the radiation dangers of Io's torus making the plane of Jupiter's magnetic equator by far the most hazardous region of the planet's magnetosphere for spacecraft to cross.

Jupiter's Satellites

Compared to their gigantic parent, the four largest satellite moons of Jupiter, the Galilean moons discovered by Galileo, seem tiny. However, if these moons existed in the region of the terrestrial planets, they would be a respectable size. Ganymede has a diameter of 3,278 miles (5,276 kilometers), which makes it larger than the planet Mercury, with its diameter of a little more than 3,031 miles (4,878 kilometers). Callisto is

Opposite: Callisto is in the foreground of this montage of Voyager images of Jupiter and its moons. Approaching the planet, the others, in order, are Ganymede, Europa and Io.

Below: Jupiter's Galilean moons follow almost circular orbits very close to the planet's equatorial plane. Unlike the other twelve known satellites of Jupiter, the Galilean moons are not "captured" asteroids, but were probably formed from the same material as the planet.

about the same size as Mercury, with a diameter of 2,995 miles (4,820 kilometers). Io is 2,256 miles (3,632 kilometers) wide, and Europa is 1,942 miles (3,126 kilometers). All except Europa are larger than our Moon, which has a diameter of 2,160 miles (3,476 kilometers).

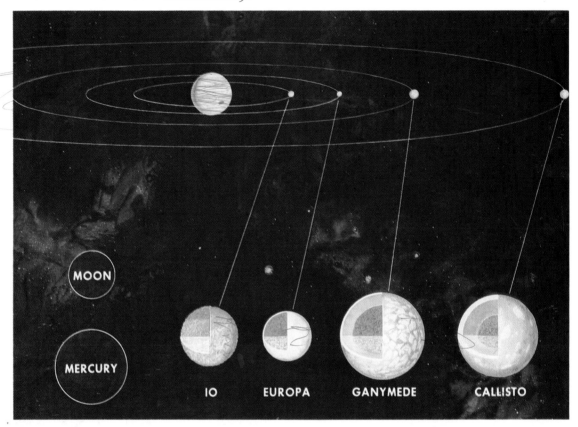

Diagram showing the size of Jupiter's moons relative to our moon and Mercury, and their orbital paths. Ganymede is larger than Mercury, and Callisto is about the same size. Only Europa is smaller than Earth's Moon.

Amalthea – Stretched Satellite

There are currently 16 known satellites of Jupiter. The four great Galilean moons are much larger than any of the others. Next in size is Amalthea, which was the first satellite of Jupiter to be discovered for almost 300 years, and the last to be sighted visually from Earth. Amalthea was discovered in 1892 by Edward Emerson Barnard. He was using the 36-inch refracting telescope at Lick Observatory on Mount Hamilton, California, on a deliberate satellite hunt. The Voyager 1 spacecraft came within 264,000 miles (425,000 kilometers) of Amalthea in March 1979. It showed that the little satellite, which is about 175 miles (280 kilometers) long and 93 miles (150 kilometers) across, always has its long axis toward Jupiter. It orbits the planet once every 12 hours or so, at a distance of 112,650 miles (181,300 kilometers). Amalthea is a dark body. It has a reddish tinge that may come from sulfur that has settled on it after being ejected from Io. Amalthea's closeness to Jupiter's enormous gravitational pull has elongated it, and it radiates more heat than it possibly could simply by reflecting warmth from Jupiter and the Sun. The planet's magnetic field may be responsible for Amalthea's unusual heat.

Close Orbits

For a long time, scientists thought that Amalthea was the closest satellite to Jupiter. However, in 1979, three small satellites were discovered on images sent back to Earth by the Voyager probes. One, known as Thebe, orbits between Amalthea and Io, about 140,000 miles (225,000 kilometers) from Jupiter. The other two, known as Metis and Adrastea, are the closest known satellites to Jupiter, orbiting at a distance of 79,785 miles (128,400 kilometers) and 79,290 miles (127,600 kilometers) respectively, well inside Amalthea's orbit.

The Inner Group

The Galileans, Amalthea, and the three little 1979 moons, which have diameters of 22 miles (35 kilometers), 47 miles (75 kilometers), and 25 miles (40 kilometers), form Jupiter's inner group of satellites. They all move in almost circular orbits in the plane of the planet's equator. Like our Moon, the Galileans have synchronous orbits, rotating once around their axes in the course of one orbit around Jupiter, so that they always present the same face to the planet. The inner satellites all move around Jupiter in a counterclockwise direction (as seen from above the planet's north pole). Of the Galileans, Io is the closest to Jupiter, at a distance

> **Did You Know?**
> Adrastea is the fastest moving moon in the Solar System. It travels at a speed of about 70,000 miles (113,600 kilometers) per hour.

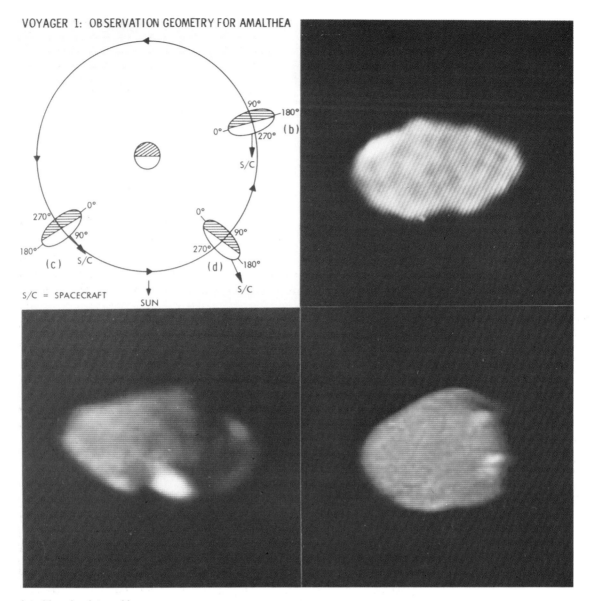

VOYAGER 1: OBSERVATION GEOMETRY FOR AMALTHEA

S/C = SPACECRAFT

Amalthea is pictured here by Voyager 1 from three different angles. It is irregular and stretched in shape and its long axis always points toward Jupiter as it orbits the planet (as shown in the inset diagram).

of 262,000 miles (421,600 kilometers); Europa is next, at a distance of 416,890 miles (670,900 kilometers); Ganymede is third, at 665,000 miles (1,070,000 kilometers); and Callisto is the farthest out, orbiting at a distance of 1,170,075 miles (1,883,000 kilometers).

Eccentric Fragments

There is a big jump from the inner group of satellites to the second group. They orbit Jupiter between 6,835,000 and 7,457,000 miles (11,000,000 and 12,000,000 kilometers) from it. There are four moons in the group. Tiny Leda has a diameter of only 6 miles (10 kilometers). Lysithea has a diameter of 15 miles (24 kilometers); Elara has a diameter of 50 miles (80 kilometers); and the largest is Himalia, with a diameter of 106 miles (170 kilometers). Like the inner group, these four orbit Jupiter in a counterclockwise direction as seen from above the planet's north pole. However, unlike the innermost group, the second group have steep orbits. They are inclined toward Jupiter's *equatorial plane,* at angles of between 26·7° and 29°. In addition, their orbits are more *eccentric*, or oval-shaped, than the almost circular orbits of the inner group. Callisto has the most eccentric orbit of the inner group, with an eccentricity of 0·0074. In the second group eccentricities vary from 0·1074 to 0·2072. They take between 254 and 276 days to orbit Jupiter.

Snared Asteroids

The outer group of satellites are named Ananke, Carme, Pasiphae, and Sinope (in order of their distances from Jupiter). All are small — between 12½ and 22 miles (20 and 36 kilometers) in diameter — and their orbits vary from 12,860,000 to 14,725,000 miles (20,700,000 to 23,700,000 kilometers) from the parent planet. Their orbits are elliptical, or oval-shaped, with eccentricities varying between 0·169 and 0·410. The orbits also lean away from the planet's equatorial plane, at angles between 147° and 163°. This takes them far above and below the orbits of the other satellites.

However, the most unusual thing about the outer group of satellites is that they all have *retrograde orbits* around Jupiter. This indicates that they almost certainly came from elsewhere in the Solar System and were captured by the planet's field of gravity. Because of their considerable distance from Jupiter, the orbits of the outer satellites are strongly affected by the gravitational pull of the Sun. They take between 631 and 758 days to circle the planet. It is likely that both the second and third groups of Jovian satellites are "captured" asteroids. Their close grouping in terms of distance from Jupiter, angle, direction and period of orbit indicates that the members of each group were all captured at about the same time. The four Galilean moons, however, were almost certainly formed at the same time, and out of the same material, as Jupiter itself.

Probes to the Planet

Most of our information about Jupiter and its system of satellites comes from the spacecraft that have made the vast journey across space from Earth to the outer planets. When the Atlas-Centaur rocket carrying the Pioneer 10 spacecraft roared away from Cape Canaveral on March 2 1972, no one knew whether man-made machines could survive the rigors and perils of interplanetary flight. For many months, it flew through regions of intense radiation, amid the threat of asteroid collision and particle bombardment.

It took 22 months for Pioneers 10 and 11 to cover the 391,000,000 miles (620,000,000 kilometers) between Earth and Jupiter. They proved that it was possible for spacecraft to cross asteroid belts and the Jovian radiation belts and still function.

This artist's impression shows Pioneer above Jupiter's Red Spot.

Pioneer 11 was launched on April 6 1973. Both craft took about 22 months to reach Jupiter. They made their *fly-bys* on December 4 1973 and December 6 1974, respectively. Pioneers 10 and 11 differed from earlier spacecraft. They could not use solar panels to provide the necessary electrical power for their systems, because they would be traveling too far from the Sun. Instead, each one was equipped with two *nuclear generators.* To lessen the danger of radiation damaging sensitive instruments, the nuclear generators were mounted on long booms, away from the body of the craft. These generators converted heat from plutonium-238 into electrical power.

Waiting for the Crash

The Pioneers also carried special equipment for detecting asteroids and meteoroids. Many scientists feared the worst as the spacecraft traversed the regions of the asteroid belt. However, the dust-sized particles in the asteroid belt caused only slight damage. It was no more severe than that experienced elsewhere in space.

The Pioneers reached Jupiter's magnetosphere a year apart. There, they encountered the bow-shock at greatly differing distances from the planet, demonstrating that the magnetosphere is extremely elastic. It expands and contracts considerably according to the varying pressure of the solar wind striking it.

New Images

The Pioneer spacecraft rotated in flight. They captured images of Jupiter, in the infrared and ultraviolet parts of the spectrum, as well as in visible light. These photographs were made in narrow strips that could then be pieced together to form a complete picture. The Pioneer television cameras, called *imaging photopolarimeters*, took pictures in both blue and red light using *prisms*, filters and mirrors. The photographs could then be combined to produce color images much clearer than those obtained from Earth-based telescopes and cameras.

Near Approaches

In December 1973, Pioneer 10's fly-bys brought it to within 81,400 miles (131,000 kilometers) of Jupiter. A year later, Pioneer 11 came as close as 28,800 miles (46,400 kilometers). Among other things, the Pioneer instruments were able to make the first accurate assessments of Jupiter's atmospheric make-up. They also measured the enormous radiation intensities encountered inside the planet's magnetosphere.

Pioneer 11 reached a top speed of 106,250 mph (171,000 km/h) and became the fastest man-made object up to that time. The craft was able to use its close fly-bys of the planet to get a *gravity-deflection* boost to take it on its way to a fly-bys of Saturn.

Voyager Blast-off

The Pioneer 10 and 11 flights were to some extent rehearsals for the far more ambitious and sophisticated Voyager flights that followed. Launched from Earth in 1977, Voyager 1 reached Jupiter in March 1979. Voyager 2 arrived in July of the same year. The Voyagers weighed 1,800 pounds (815 kilograms) apiece. Each one was equipped with an on-board computer system, as well as three nuclear generators to provide electrical power.

The year 1977 was very good for the Voyager launches. An alignment of planets that occurs only once every 176 years allowed scientists to plan an ambitious exploration program. Visits to Jupiter, Saturn,

Voyager 1 pictures were used to construct this view of Jupiter's northern hemisphere from directly above the pole, showing the clearly-defined belt-like layers that reach to the poles.

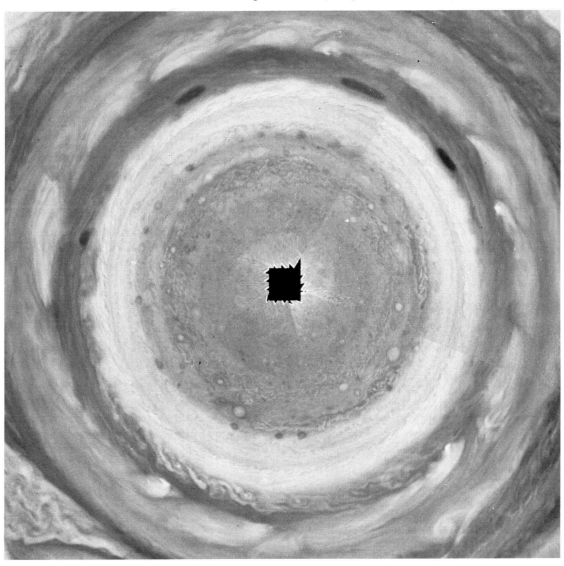

and Neptune were involved, using gravity-assisted boosts for each stage of the journey.

Computers in Space

The Voyager cameras were an improvement over those in Pioneer 10 and 11. Instead of thin strips of image taken as the spacecraft rotated, the Voyagers' shuttered cameras produced images composed of 640,000 *pixels,* or picture cells, each. Each of these tiny picture elements can be measured for brightness and can then be stored in the computer's memory, or transmitted back to Earth.

Both of the Voyager spacecraft made close studies of the Galilean moons, as well as scanning the planet closely and taking remarkable new pictures of its tur-

The four Galilean moons of Jupiter present sharply differing faces to the observer: the volcanic deposits of Io, the ice cracks of Europa, the deep valleys of Ganymede, and the ancient craters of Callisto.

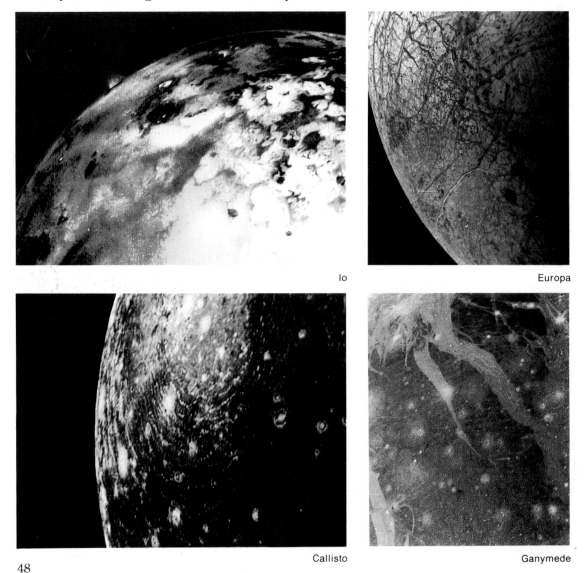

Io

Europa

Callisto

Ganymede

bulent atmosphere. They were also able to take a close look at the irregular shape of Amalthea for the first time.

Rings of Jupiter

New discoveries included the three tiny satellites, Metis, Thebe and Adrastea, and, most surprising of all, Jupiter's rings. Scientists had no idea that Jupiter had rings, similar to, but much thinner and smaller than, those of Saturn. Voyager 1 sent back the first images of Jupiter's ring system; Voyager 2 was then programed to take additional pictures. Jupiter's rings are made of tiny particles. They extend out more than 35,400 miles (57,000 kilometers) from Jupiter's cloud tops. The thin disk, with a maximum thickness of half a mile (one kilometer), reaches almost all the way to the planet

Voyager 1 astonished the scientific world when it sent back the first evidence of Jupiter's ring system, formed of tiny particles visible only when they are lit from behind by the Sun.

at its inner diameter. The particles forming the rings are so small that they only become visible when they are lit from behind by the Sun. The main concentration of ring particles forms a band about 4,000 miles (6,500 kilometers) wide. The particles are probably fine dust. They may have come from a small satellite which broke up because of gravitational disruption. Other material originating from meteorite debris and volcanic dust from Io may also be present.

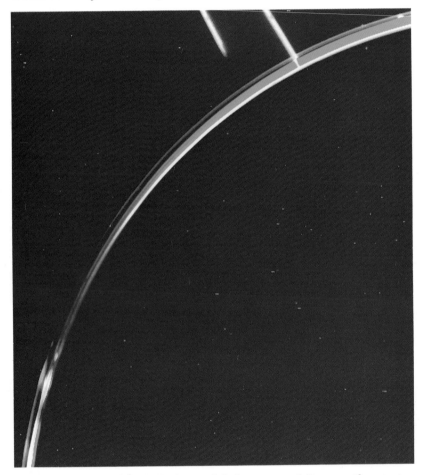

Jupiter's ring system is shown in this composite picture, which was made using two color filters, which are visible as two light colored lines protruding from the top. The ring system has a main band 4,000 miles (6,500 kilometers) wide, and a fainter disk stretching all the way to the planet's atmosphere. It loses particles constantly, possibly replenishing them with material shed by moon Io.

The tiny satellites Metis and Adrastea orbit near the outer edge of the ring. They seem to have a definite role in shaping the ring. They appear to "sweep up" particles, giving the outer edge its very clean-cut, sharply-defined profile.

Volcanic Moon

Some of the most fascinating information from the Voyager flights came from their close examination of the Galilean moons. On Friday, March, 9, 1979, Linda Morabito, a navigation engineer at the Jet Propulsion

This composite picture is made from four different images taken on March 4 1979, with different light filters. It clearly shows a volcanic eruption on Io billowing out from the moon's horizon, 175 miles (280 kilometers) into space.

Laboratory in California where NASA has its Deep Space Communications Complex, was checking a Voyager 1 image of Io. While increasing the brightness on her computer screen, she suddenly discovered a great spouting plume rising 280 kilometers (175 miles) above Io's surface. Morabito had become the first person ever to see an erupting volcano anywhere beyond the planet Earth. The news startled the scientific community, who had never found proof of geologically active worlds beyond our own. A concentrated search soon turned up a number of erupting volcanoes on Io.

Voyager 1 had shown Io to have a warmly-colored red and yellow-orange surface. The moon's crust is probably constructed of sulfur and sulfur dioxide, which would account for the colors. Internally, Io is thought to have a solid central core surrounded by molten silicates.

Io was the first body beyond Earth in the Solar System discovered to have active volcanoes. Its surface is covered with volcanic debris, vents and lava plains.

Satellite Under Stress

Io's volcanism is probably the result of its position as the innermost large satellite. It orbits Jupiter at a distance of 421,600 kilometers (261,975 miles) every 42½ hours. It is subjected to gravitational pulls from the planet and from Europa, the next moon out. These gravitational pulls exert a powerful "flexing" force on

This view of Io, taken by Voyager 1 from 266,000 miles (364,000 kilometers) away, shows its pizza-like surface, with red, sulfurous, volcanic deposits and dark vent sites.

Below: Voyager 1 took these images of two separate active volcanic events on Io. Pictures a, b, and c show the vent and two eruption angles of one volcano, while picture d shows the vent of another. Pictures e and f show this vent in action.

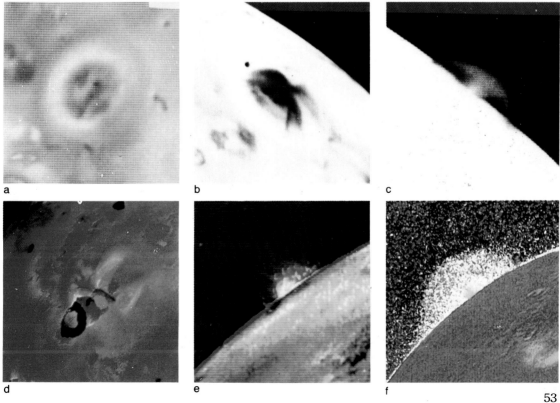

a

b

c

d

e

f

53

Io's structure. They result in increased internal heating, and the pressures lead to volcanic eruptions. The power of these eruptions shoots molten material hundreds of miles above the moon's surface, with a force many times greater than anything experienced in volcanoes on Earth.

Since the Voyager flights, Earth-based astronomers have seen volcanic activity on Io, using NASA's Infrared Telescope Facility on Hawaii. With the aid of a new *infrared camera* called a ProtoCAM, scientists on Hawaii discovered a previously unknown erupting volcano in late 1989, to add to the nine already captured in the Voyager images.

Speedy Europa

Europa orbits Jupiter once every 3·5 days at a distance of 416,890 miles (670,900 kilometers). It orbits Jupiter at almost twice the speed of Io. As a result, the two moons are frequently in conjunction, forming a straight line with the planet. The regular gravitational influence of Europa prevents Io from moving into a more circular orbit which might lessen the constant gravitational wrenching which Io receives from Jupiter. Europa's density, 3·3 times that of water, indicates that, like Io, it has a solid silicate core. The Voyager probes showed that Europa has an unusually smooth, whitish surface, with some dark patches, and a complex network of dark lines.

Ancient Floods

The bright, reflective surface of Europa is almost certainly made of ice or frost, and the dark criss-crossing lines may be cracks in the ice. The "tidal" gravitational forces that heat up the interior of Io have far less effect

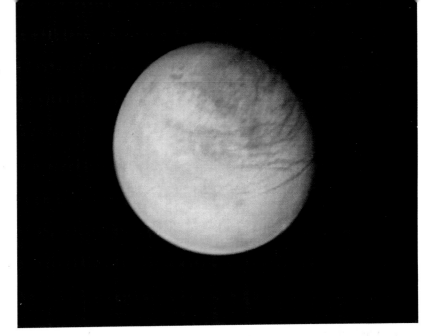

The moon Europa appears as a world of thick, fractured ice-crusts over a rocky core. Its surface is bright with ice and almost free of craters.

on Europa, but are still probably strong enough to keep an interior body of water in a liquid, or semi-liquid, ice-slush state. The almost total absence of impact craters puzzles astronomers, but could be explained if water had, at some time in the past, flooded up from

A closer look at Europa reveals a network of dark fissures criss-crossing its surface. These ice valleys are up to 25 miles (40 kilometers) wide and thousands of kilometers long, and were possibly caused by underground movement.

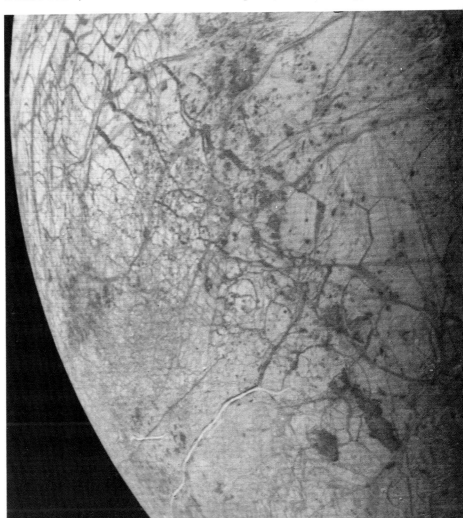

the interior to cover the surface in a frozen layer. Dirty water welling up between cracks in the ice-crust could be the source of the dark lines on the moon's surface.

Ganymede – Biggest and Brightest

Ganymede is the third largest satellite in the Solar System, after Saturn's Titan and Neptune's Triton. The largest of Jupiter's moons, it has a diameter of 5,276

Ganymede, Jupiter's largest moon, shows heavily cratered dark areas of ancient origin. Brighter regions of grooved terrain bear more recent craters. Tectonic movements may have caused the grooves.

kilometers (3,279 miles) and orbits the planet at a distance of 1,070,000 kilometers (665,000 miles) once every 7 days 4 hours of Earth time.

Ganymede is also the brightest of the Galilean moons. Its *albedo* (reflectiveness) of 0·4 reveals the high percentage of ice in its make-up. This high proportion is confirmed by the moon's low density, just under twice that of water. Ganymede is probably about half rock and half water or ice.

Patchwork of Old and New

Ganymede was closely and comprehensively mapped by the Voyager instruments. The transmitted pictures reveal a world with a patchy light and dark surface. The dark patches indicate ancient areas of ice, heavily pitted with old craters. The light areas consist of newer ice, still ridged and grooved into a deep-valleyed terrain that shows the effects of surface and underground movements. On the darker, older areas, the surface features have sunk into smoothness. Ganymede probably once had an active geological system, with icy continents slowly sliding and colliding, powered by convection currents from an unknown source.

Cratered Callisto

Farthest out of the Galileans, at a distance of 1,883,000 kilometers (1,170,000 miles) from Jupiter, Callisto takes almost seventeen days to complete its orbit. This dark moon is densely pocked with craters in its thick icy crust. It has a low density, about 1·6 times that of water. Scientists think that it has a mantle of soft ice or water about 625 miles (1,000 kilometers) deep around its silicate core.

Callisto shows its heavily cratered surface in this Voyager 2 image of July 1979, taken at a distance of 677,000 miles (1,000,000 kilometers). Bright markings indicate craters where underground water, released by the impact, has frozen on the surface.

Beneath the mantle there appears to be an icy, rocky crust that could be as much as 300 kilometers (185 miles) deep.

Battered Moon

At some point in the distant past, Callisto was struck by a vast meteorite. It left an impact region of concentric

Above: Seen against the blackness of space, the Galileo spacecraft is detached from its cradle-like device aboard the Earth-orbiting space shuttle Atlantis to begin its six-year journey to Jupiter. The Earth's horizon and atmosphere can be seen on the left of this picture.

Right: On October 18 1989, Galileo finally got underway after years of delays. It climbed into space aboard the Atlantis space shuttle and was released at an altitude of 185 miles (298 kilometers).

ripples now called Valhalla, 1,850 miles (3,000 kilometers) across. The impact may have almost penetrated Callisto's thick crust. Callisto's surface record is very ancient, showing that the moon has been geologically inactive for billions of years.

There could be more moons of Jupiter than the 16 that scientists have so far discovered. Any others would, however, have to be very small to have avoided the instruments and eyes of the Pioneer and Voyager teams. The Jovian system is in some ways like a Solar System in miniature, though Jupiter is certainly a planet and not a star. The great Galilean moons are as fascinating as the planets themselves. Both they and the gas giant that is their parent planet are still full of secrets to be revealed by future space explorations.

Books to Read

INTRODUCTORY READING

Cosmic Quest: Searching for Intelligent Life Among the Stars by Margaret Poynter and
  Michael J. Klein (Macmillan, 1984)

Extraterrestrials by Isaac Asimov (Harper and Row Junior Books, 1988)

The Giant Planets by Alan E. Nurse (Franklin Watts, 1982)

Jupiter by Simon Seymore (William Morrow, 1988)

Jupiter: The Spotted Giant by Isaac Asimov (Gareth Stephens Inc., 1989)

Mysteries of Life On Earth and Beyond by Franklyn M. Branley (Lodestar Books, 1987)

Mysteries of the Planets by Franklyn M. Branley (Lodestar Books, 1988)

Other Worlds: Is There Life Out There? by David J. Darling (Dillon Press, 1985)

Planets by Norman Barrett (Franklin Watts, 1984)

The Planets by Jonathan Rutland (Random House, 1987)

Rockets and Satellites by Francene Sabin (Troll Associates, 1985)

Satellites and Computers by Mat Irvine (Franklin Watts, 1984)

Space Sciences by Christopher Lampton (Franklin Watts, 1984)

Spaceprobes and Satellites by Heather Couper and Nigel Henbest
  (Franklin Watts, 1987)

The Story of Apollo II by Conrad Stein (Children's Press, 1985)

FURTHER READING

America's Astronauts and Their Indestructible Spirit by Fred Kelly (TAB Books, 1986)

The Cambridge Atlas of Astronomy edited by Jean Audouze and Guy Israel
  (Cambridge University Press, 1988)

Challenge of the Spaceship by Arthur C. Clark (Pocket Books, 1980)

Diary of a Cosmonaut: Two Hundred and Eleven Days in Space by Valentin Lbedev
  (Phyto Resource Research, 1988)

In Darkness Born: The Story of Star Formation by Martin Cohen
  (Cambridge University Press, 1988)

Interiors of the Planets by A. H. Cook (Cambridge University Press, 1981)

Interstellar Matters by G. L. Verschuur (Springer-Verlag New York, 1988)

Jupiter: King of the Gods, Giant of the Planets by Franklyn M. Branley
  (Lodestar Books, 1981)

Jupiter: The Star That Failed by Joel N. Shurkin (Westminster/John Knox
  Press, 1979)

Lifesearch by Time-Life Books Editors (Time-Life, 1989)

Glossary

ALBEDO The reflectiveness of a body, expressed as a percentage of sunlight reaching it.

APHELION The point in a planet's orbit when it is furthest from the Sun.

ASTEROID A minor planet, or planetoid, orbiting the Sun. Most asteroids orbit in a "belt" between the orbits of Mars and Jupiter.

BOW-SHOCK The region where a planet's magnetosphere meets the solar wind.

CENTRIFUGAL FORCE The force exerted outward from the radius of a spinning body.

CURRENT SHEET A flattened disk of charged particles rotating approximately in the plane of Jupiter's magnetic equator.

DECAMETRIC RADIATION Radio emissions from Jupiter which occur in irregular bursts at wavelengths of more than 25 feet (7·5 meters).

DECIMETRIC RADIATION An even, continuous radio emission from Jupiter at wavelengths between 2 inches (5 centimeters) and 10 feet (3 meters).

DIFFERENTIATION Process early in a planet's formation by which the denser elements, often metallic, sink to form a core, while lighter material forms the outer layers.

ECCENTRIC ORBIT An orbit that is not circular.

EQUATORIAL PLANE The theoretical plane extending through the equator of a planet.

ESCAPE VELOCITY The minimum speed necessary for any object to escape a particular gravitational field.

FLY-BY An observational flight by a spacecraft that passes close to a planet or satellite.

GALILEAN MOONS The four largest moons of Jupiter, discovered by Galileo.

GAS GIANT One of the outer planets Jupiter, Saturn, Uranus and Neptune, which are composed principally of gases.

GRAVITY DEFLECTION The technique of "skipping" a spacecraft off a planet's gravitational field to speed it on its way.

IMAGING PHOTOPOLARIMETER A scanning telescope fitted with instruments to analyse the polarization of light and linked to TV-type cameras.

INFRARED CAMERA A camera which records images from infrared emanations, between the radio and visible bands of the electromagnetic spectrum.

MAGNETIC AXIS The imaginary line through the magnetic poles of a planet or satellite.

MAGNETIC FLUX TUBE A loop of magnetic field lines connecting the moon Io to Jupiter, which cause bursts of radio noise.

MAGNETOPAUSE The outer boundary of a planet's magnetosphere outside which is the magnetosheath.

MAGNETOSHEATH The region of turbulence between a planet's magnetosphere and its bow-shock.

MAGNETOSPHERE The envelope around a planet in which its magnetic field has significant effect.

MAGNETOTAIL The tail of a planet's magnetosphere, carried "downstream" by the solar wind.

METALLIC HYDROGEN A form of liquid hydrogen that exists under conditions of great pressure and heat, and which is found only in the gas giant planets and in the Sun and stars.

METEROID Pieces of rock or metal that are present in outer space. Most are very small. Those that enter Earth's atmosphere (and burn up) are known as meteors. Those that reach the ground are meteorites.

NUCLEAR GENERATOR Electrical generator on space probes going to Jupiter and beyond, which converts heat from the radioactive decay of certain elements into electrical power.

PERIHELION The point of closest approach of an orbiting planet to the Sun.

PIXEL A small computer image used to build pictures on visual display screens.

PRISM A translucent device with intersecting plane surfaces that can separate "white" light into its color spectrum.

RAD A unit for measuring the dose of radiation absorbed by any material.

RADIO FREQUENCY MAP The image of a region or body created from recordings of its radio emissions.

RETROGRADE ORBIT A clockwise orbital motion, as seen from the north pole of a planet. Most Solar Systems orbits are counterclockwise.

THERMAL RADIATION Electromagnetic radiation emitted from a heat source.

TORUS A "ring doughnut" shape, like the plasma torus around Jupiter following Io's orbit.

Looking at the Planets

Jupiter is at opposition every thirteen months, and you can easily pick out its disk with binoculars. With a telescope, you may even see some or all of its four Galilean moons. Jupiter takes about a year to move through one zodiacal constellation and 12 years to make a complete orbit of the Sun. An almanac will tell you in which constellation Jupiter lies.

Jupiter is very bright, three times as bright as Sirius, the brightest star, and should be easy to find with the use of a star chart. The planet shines a steady yellow. The Galilean moons show as bright points of light, moving within the thin line of the planet's equatorial plane as they orbit.

A × 20 telescope will allow you to see that Jupiter is slightly flattened, but you will need a higher magnification to see the zones in the planet's atmosphere.

Index